Cathy
and
Emma

love
Jessica

2001

Bundle of Joy

A Precious Gift

Compiled by Phyllis D'Aprile Alston

Illustrated by Valerie Morone

PETER PAUPER PRESS, INC.
WHITE PLAINS, NEW YORK

*For my bundles of joy, Rodney, Jr.
and Tiffanie Rose, and for my
mother, Rosemary, for making me
her bundle of joy.*

Copyright © 1995
Peter Pauper Press, Inc.
202 Mamaroneck Avenue
White Plains, NY 10601
All rights reserved
ISBN 0-88088-772-9
Printed in China
7

Bundle of Joy

Name _____

Birth Date _____ Time _____

Weight _____

Birthplace/Hospital _____

_____

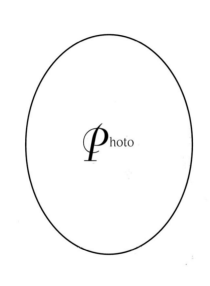

$\mathcal{P}$hoto

Bundle of Joy

A baby is an angel whose wings
decrease as his legs increase.

FRENCH PROVERB

*B*abies are necessary to grown-ups. A new baby is like the beginning of all things—wonder, hope, a dream of possibilities… babies are almost the only remaining link with nature, with the natural world of living things from which we spring.

EDA J. LeShan

I do not know how you appeared in my womb; it was not I who endowed you with breath and life. I had not the shaping of your every part. It is the creator of the world, ordaining the process of man's birth and presiding over the origin of all things…

2 Maccabees, 7:22, 23

*I*s it hard to imagine what your family will be like with a new baby there? Just as you can have plenty of love for both your mom and dad, they can have plenty of love for both you *and* the new baby.

MR. ROGERS

*M*y mother groan'd, my father wept,
Into the dangerous world I leapt;
Helpless, naked, piping loud,
Like a fiend hid in a cloud.

WILLIAM BLAKE

Raising children is like baking bread; it has to be a slow process or you end up with an overdone crust and an underdone interior.

Marcelene Cox

*B*abies are always more trouble than you thought—and more wonderful.

CHARLES OSGOOD

A baby is an inestimable blessing and bother.

MARK TWAIN

*T*he only reason you were born was to be better than your parents and to make this world better for your children.

DREW BROWN

I have never understood the fear of some parents about babies getting mixed up in the hospital. What difference does it make as long as you get a good one?

HEYWOOD BROUN

You can sort of be married, you can sort of be divorced, you can sort of be living together, but you can't sort of have a baby.

DAVID SHIRE

*H*aving a baby is like falling in love again, both with your husband and your child.

TINA BROWN

*B*abies, babies, babies. I love them. No matter how I feel they always brighten up my day!

PHYLLIS D'APRILE ALSTON

*T*he art of being a parent is to sleep
when the baby isn't looking.

ANONYMOUS

*T*he great high of Wimbledon lasts for about a week. You do go down in the record books, but you don't have anything tangible to hold on to. But having a baby—there just isn't any comparison.

CHRIS EVERT

*T*ruth, which is important to a scholar, has got to be concrete. And there is nothing more concrete than dealing with babies, burps and bottles, frogs and mud!

JEANE J. KIRKPATRICK

*A*mong the three or four million cradles now rocking in the land are some which this nation would preserve for ages as sacred things, if we could know which ones they are.

MARK TWAIN

*T*he joys of parents are secret,
and so are their griefs and fears.

FRANCIS BACON

A perfect example of minority rule
is a baby in the house.

MILWAUKEE JOURNAL

*B*abies are unreasonable; they
expect far too much of existence.
Each new generation that comes
takes one look at the world, thinks
wildly, "Is *this* all they've done to it?"
and bursts into tears.

CLARENCE DAY

*A*bout the only thing we have left that actually discriminates in favor o' the plain people is the stork.

KIN HUBBARD

Sweet bud of promise, fresh and fair,
  Just moving in the morning air.
The morn of life but just begun.
The sands of time just set to run!
Sweet babe with cheek of pinky hue.
With eyes of soft ethereal blue,
With raven hair like finest down
Of unfledged bird, and scant'ly shown
Beneath the cap of cumbrous lace,

That circles round thy placid face!
Ah, baby! little dost thou know
How many yearning bosoms glow,
How many lips in blessings move,
How many eyes beam looks of love
At sight of thee!

JOANNA BAILLIE

*T*here is nothing as ancient as infancy. Unchanging ancientness is born into homes again and again in the form of a baby, yet the freshness, beauty, innocence and sweetness it had at the beginning of history is the same today.

RABINDRANATH TAGORE

*B*abies don't need vacations,
but I still see them at the beach.

STEVEN WRIGHT

We all of us wanted babies—but did we want children?

EDA J. LESHAN

What are little girls made of?
What are little girls made of?
Sugar and spice and all things nice,
And such are little girls made of.

SOUTHEY

What are little boys made of, made of?
What are little boys made of?
Snips and snails and puppy-dog tails,
And such are little boys made of.

SOUTHEY

*E*very baby born into the world
is a finer one than the last.

CHARLES DICKENS

A boy is a magical creature—
you can lock him out of your
workshop, but you can't lock him
out of your heart.

ALLAN BECK

A girl is Innocence playing in the mud, Beauty standing on its head, and Motherhood dragging a doll by the foot.

ALLAN BECK

*P*at-a-cake, pat-a-cake, baker's man,
   Bake me a cake as fast as you can;
Pat it and prick it, and mark it with B,
Put it in the oven for baby and me.

Nursery Rhyme

*M*y heart leaps when I look into the face of my beautiful Indian child, wrapped in the strength of his father's arms: together we are the flag of North America. We are growing free and joyous.

BUFFY SAINTE-MARIE

*T*here is no finer investment for any community than putting milk into babies.

WINSTON CHURCHILL

Sweetest li'l feller, everybody knows;
Dunno what you call him, but
he's mighty lak' a rose.

FRANK L. STANTON

*S*omething to live for came to the place.
Something to die for maybe,
Something to give even sorrow a grace.
And yet it was only a baby!

LOUISE MOULTON

*B*egin, baby boy, to recognize your mother with a smile.

VIRGIL

*B*abies hardly take any space at all. They are only about 21 inches long.

SUE TOWNSEND

_W_hen I was born I was so
surprised I didn't talk for a
year and a half.

GRACIE ALLEN

*B*ye baby bunting,
  Daddy's gone a-hunting.
Gone to get a rabbit skin
To wrap the baby bunting in.

NURSERY RHYME

Where did you come from, baby dear?
Out of the everywhere into here.

GEORGE MacDONALD

*N*owadays babies get up and walk soon's you drop 'em, but twenty years ago when I was a girl babies stayed babies longer.

TONI MORRISON

*D*o not try to produce an ideal child;
it would find no fitness in this world.

HERBERT SPENCER

*I*f people ask me when I began to dance I reply, "In my mother's womb, probably as a result of the oysters and champagne—the food of Aphrodite."

ISADORA DUNCAN

*T*here's just a closeness and a security that you're there. I didn't care that I was awakened two to three times a night and still had to get up at six o'clock in the morning and go to work.

DEMI MOORE

When the first baby laughed for the first time, the laugh broke into a thousand pieces and they all went skipping about, and that was the beginning of fairies.

JAMES M. BARRIE,
Peter Pan

I'll do anything but the 2 a.m. feeding. There's only one area I'll try to influence. She'll be an Angels fan.

RICHARD NIXON,
*on the birth of his first grandchild,
Jennie Eisenhower*

*M*y daughter is sort of light-years ahead of anything else of the priorities in my life.

CANDICE BERGEN

*L*ittle girls are the nicest things
that happen to people.

ALLAN BECK

I'd love to have a little girl with a ponytail and a two-handed backhand to remind me of Chrissie.

ANDY MILL

I don't want him to lose his first tooth or outgrow his little diapers. This will be one slow-growth baby.

DEIDRE HALL

I keep waiting for him to speak. I want him to either lean over and play the piano or show extraordinary technical skills.

HOWARD STRINGER

A newborn baby is an extraordinary event; and I have never seen two babies who looked exactly alike. Here is the breathing miracle who could not live an instant without you, with a skull more fragile than an egg, a miracle of eyes, legs, toenails, and lungs.

JAMES BALDWIN

Our children…are not treated with sufficient respect as human beings, and yet from the moment they are born they have this right to respect. We keep them children far too long, their world separate from the real world of life.

PEARL S. BUCK

*T*here are one hundred and fifty-two distinctly different ways of holding a baby—and all are right.

HEYWOOD BROUN

*T*here is only one genuine
misfortune, not to be born.

JOAQUIM MACHADO DE ASSIS

*T*his is my beloved Son, in whom I am well pleased.

MATTHEW 3:17

*T*here was a little girl
Who had a little curl
Right in the middle of her forehead,
And when she was good
She was very, very good,
And when she was bad she was horrid.

HENRY WADSWORTH LONGFELLOW

*T*here is nothing like a start, and being born, however pessimistic one may become in later years, is undeniably a start.

WILLIAM MCFEE

My lovely living boy,
My hope, my hap, my love,
my life, my joy.

SIR EDWARD DYER

*T*here's only one pretty baby in the world, and every mother has it.

PROVERB

"Sir—sir, it is a boy!" "A boy," said my father, looking up from his book, and evidently much puzzled; "what is a boy?"

E. G. Bulwer-Lytton,
The Caxtons

*H*ow many hopes and fears,
how many ardent wishes and
anxious apprehensions are twisted
together in the threads that connect
the parent with the child!

SAMUEL GRISWOLD GOODRICH

Sleep, baby, sleep!
  Thy father's watching the sheep,
Thy mother's shaking the dreamland tree,
And down drops a little dream for thee.
Sleep, baby, sleep.

ELIZABETH PRENTISS
Cradle Song